when Tragedy Strikes

CHARLES STANLEY

THOMAS NELSON PUBLISHERS®
Nashville

A Division of Thomas Nelson, Inc.

Published by Thomas Nelson, Inc.

Scripture quotations are taken from THE NEW AMERICAN STANDARD BIBLE ®, Copyright © The Lockman Foundation™ 1960, 1962, 1963, 1968, 1971, 1972, 1973, 1975, 1977. Used by permission.

ISBN 0-7852-6544-9

Printed in the United States of America

Dedicated to all the families
who lost loved ones in the September 11, 2001,
terrorist attacks.

Contents

Psalm 27:1–3

The Lord is my light and my salvation;
    Whom shall I fear?
The Lord is the defense of my life;
    Whom shall I dread?
When evildoers came upon me to devour
    my flesh,
My adversaries and my enemies,
    they stumbled and fell.
Though a host encamp against me,
    My heart will not fear;
Though war rise against me,
    In spite of this I shall be confident.

Introduction

Hidden away on the third page of our newspaper today is the story of thirteen miners who died at the Blue Creek No. 5 mine in Brookwood, Alabama. Apparently there was an initial explosion, and three miners were trapped, injured, or killed. Ten other miners immediately went into the mine to try and rescue their stricken colleagues. While seeking their friends to give them aid, another explosion occurred, and all thirteen men lost their lives.

I suppose this story would have grabbed front-page headlines on a "normal" day but these days are anything but normal. We are faced with death and destruction as has never before been experienced in America. The enormity of the disaster that ensued as a result of the attacks in New York and Washington, D.C. makes other tragic moments in the day-to-day affairs of our nation pale in comparison. The pain and heartache stemming from all types of disasters is very real, and no matter how small or localized the circumstance, it affects deeply all of those who are involved. That being said, we do not make light of any situation that leaves people in grief.

Tragedy affects all cultures and societies. Sooner or later, every person will be faced with the sadness and difficulties associated with a sudden traumatic event that will change forever life as they know it. And tragedy comes in different shapes and sizes. Individuals, families, cities, regions, and nations experience horrifying disasters. And, as in the case of the attacks on the World Trade Center and the Pentagon, some tragic events affect the entire world.

In recent memory we recall massive damaging earthquakes in Turkey and Mexico that took many lives. We shudder at the thought of hundreds killed in religious warfare in Northern Ireland and Indonesia. Some of us recall our sense of disquiet that occurred during the nuclear meltdown in Chernobyl. And what can we say regarding the school shootings in Colorado and Kentucky?

Frankly, dear reader, tragedies come and go—they are part of our daily existence. But almost always they occur with such devastating *abruptness*. We get the phone call about the auto accident. We hear of the heart attack. We catch the quick flash on the evening news about ships colliding on the high seas with the where-abouts of the crew unknown.

Most of the time we are stunned by what we see and hear. Sometimes, however, many of us seem to be immune to the sudden news events that should change our status-quo feelings and galvanize us to action but which, in reality, find many apathetic and unmoved by the trauma.

We are children of an age in which tragedy has become part of our daily agenda. Most of the time tragic events are not something for which we plan. We do not arrange ahead of time to face these sudden crisis moments in our lives, unless, of course, our professional respon-sibilities direct that we are part of some type of emergency-management team whose specific responsibility is to prepare for such disasters.

This past week, I heard an interview with an emergency room physician in Washington,

D.C. He described how, in his capacity as chief of disaster preparation for the hospital, the systems he had put into place seemed to work quite adequately as they began bringing in the wounded from the Pentagon attack. Nevertheless, he commented that in spite of all the advance planning, there were many unforeseen situations that became apparent to them as they were flooded with the victims of the disaster. Also, he wondered aloud as to what they would have done if their hospital had been the target of such a terrorist attack.

CHANGED FOREVER

Even the word "tragedy" in our language seems to convey a sense of foreboding and fearful anticipation. So, it is no surprise that the events that have happened in our nation in the most recent past have stung all of us to the core. We've had many, many different kinds of emotions—disbelief, revenge, rage, frustration, and fear, to name but a few. In my judgment, however, no single historical event since the Civil War has caused us to recoil with such horror and to view a terrorist attack with so much individual and national anger.

It may well be that our nation will be changed forever. The President implied as much when he said, "Our war on terrorism will not end until every terrorist group of global reach has been found, stopped, and defeated," as quoted in *U.S. News and World Report* from October 1, 2001. War has come to us. In all the other wars we have taken part in, we have fought to protect our own interests or to help others in their struggles on foreign territory. But now, for the first time, we have been attacked on our own soil—and in such a despicable manner.

Somebody might ask the question, "Why would you say this is the most horrendous, tragic event in our nation's history dating back to the Civil War?" For one simple reason: this tragedy was the result of a planned, premeditated, clandestine guerilla operation designed to destroy the lives of thousands of innocent people. Hate and bigotry motivated it, and worst of all, it was cloaked in religious fervor. That fact alone makes it horrific!

This was the evil work of evil men whose minds were darkened to the point of believing that they could indiscriminately maim and murder thousands of people and be rewarded by their god. These were actions stemming from depraved minds, minds with no sense of shame or conscience that purposed to create mayhem and havoc in America by destroying multitudes of innocent people.

This was neither a simple, causal action nor a spur-of-the-moment afterthought. Rather, it represented a fundamental decision by terrorists to attack America, which they call the "Great Satan." They believed they were fulfilling a Koranic injunction to declare war on "the infidels." It did not take our nation's leaders and the nation as a whole much time to see clearly that these terrorists' actions represented an act of war against our country.

THE LORD IS THE DEFENSE
OF MY LIFE

Some of us who are old enough recall how difficult it can be to live during trying times, to face an enemy seeking to destroy all that is held sacred and dear. In such times people seek help, comfort, assurance, and safety. In moments of tragedy and crisis there is no better place to turn than to our God who has promised to help those who turn to Him in times of trouble. Yes, it is time for us to look up and seek our God, and to ask Him for words of comfort and strength for our hearts.

Many of God's saints have known times of trouble and difficulty as they journeyed through life. Consider David the psalmist of Israel. Though he was anointed and chosen to be king, he found himself hated and hunted by those who sought to destroy him. In Psalm 27, however, notice what he says while in the midst of trouble:

> The Lord is [the] light [of] my salvation; Whom shall I fear?

The Lord is the defense of my life; Whom shall
    I dread?
When evildoers came upon me to devour my
    flesh,
My adversaries and my enemies,
    they stumbled and fell.
Though a host encamp against me, my heart
    will not fear;
Though war rise against me, In spite of this I
    shall be confident. (vv. 1–3, emphasis added)

These are the words of a man who has learned how to be sustained in the most difficult, trying times of life. He learned an amazing lesson—in the midst of tragedy, he did not need to live in fear, because God was his defense. Though in a war zone, he could be fully confident that God would *protect and sustain* him

There is hope for us because God has promised never to leave us or to forsake us. There is hope because we are not alone—we have each other. This is the strength of a nation under attack—a united spirit gaining confidence and determination from each other. But more importantly, learning to rely on our God.

President George W. Bush, in his speech before the nation, said, "This country will define our times, not be defined by them." In other words he was telling the American people that it is critically important for us to decide how we are going to respond to this attack. We were unprepared for it, but now we are to actively decide what we must do. How should we respond to this tragedy?

Make no mistake, this is a critical moment for us all. To a great extent how we respond will affect and determine much of the future for us. In some ways our response to tragedy—

whether it is personal and limited in effect or a large-scale national crisis such as the one we now face—should be the same. I want to focus on the country as a whole with the understanding that the truth stated will be applicable in all tragic circumstances.

1

Compassion and Concern

How should we respond when, like a bolt out of the blue, our cherished ideals, our family's safety, our future security, and all the other dreams of life for which we have labored and invested much time and effort are suddenly threatened? As I pondered and prayed about this question it became clear to me that there are some answers.

First, *we should respond with compassion and concern for those who are suffering and for those who are hurt.* Do you recall your feelings when you saw those planes fly into the World Trade Center towers? The scenes of people clinging to windows desperately hoping to

3

escape the inferno engulfing their offices. All those tragic moments were muted, however, when we saw the buildings implode and collapse. Thousands of workers and helpers buried beneath the rubble. Can life ever return to normal again? Some people have used the word "surreal" to describe these images, as though they were make-believe scenes from a movie.

How long did it take you to realize that you had entered a new world—one in which things would never be the same for you as an American citizen? Have you been able to give satisfactory explanations to your children about this tragedy? Will the ugly head of post-traumatic stress syndrome manifest itself again as it did after the Vietnam War? How long it will be before the children of those innocent victims display the symptoms that so often accompany sudden tragedies such as this? Yes, we are in the midst of a dark, bleak period in our nation's history—but there is hope.

Gordon MacDonald, a pastor and former president of InterVarsity Christian Fellowship, spent a week with the Salvation Army relief teams at the rescue site where the World Trade Center towers collapsed. He and his wife, Gail, worked in horrific conditions from morning to night at "Ground Zero." MacDonald writes: "No church service, no church sanctuary, no religiously inspiring service has spoke so deeply into my soul and witnessed to the presence of God as those hours last night at the crash site."

"In all my years of Christian ministry, as much as I love preaching the Bible and all the other things that I have been privileged to do over the years, being on that street, giving cold water to workmen, praying and weeping with them, listening to their stories was the closest I have ever felt to God. Even though it sounds melodramatic, I kept finding myself saying, 'This is the place where Jesus most wants to be.'"

Friends, when we see God at work through compassionate, caring deeds and when we sense His presence through the caring hands of others, then we can face the future with a degree of confidence that would be utterly lacking and absent from us if we stood alone.

GROUND ZERO

At the time of my writing this, thousands of workers from all over America are still clambering over the debris at the crash site wanting and desperately willing some of those who may still be trapped under the rubble to be found and saved. It has been days since the actual crash, and most everyone believes now that there is little hope for finding anyone still alive, yet these valiant rescuers toil on, day and night. They have assumed the responsibility of doing what they can. And *so must we.* We must offer aid, comfort, and compassion to those who have been traumatized by these events.

A few days ago, I was in Manhattan at "Ground Zero" to bring comfort and solace, to be a helping presence for God and good in a place of indescribable horror and suffering. I will never be the same. No one visiting the crash site, that scene of devastation and destruction, could remain unchanged. To some degree, though, all of us were visitors there—in spirit if not in body—through the news footage that we saw.

Since the advent of television we are no longer onlookers or passersby, we have become part of ongoing events, players in the action. This medium is able to affect us deeply and to ignite compassion in us as we see how others have been affected. This is a good thing. But there must be more; there must be a greater role for us to play than that of being deeply touched by what we see and hear on television. So, what is our responsibility?

BECOME A COMFORTER

When we go through adversity it is so reassuring to have someone there to walk with us. It is so comforting to know our God is "the Father of all comfort" who has promised never to leave us or to forsake us. One of the simple things that we can do in the midst of tragedy is to reach out to people with compassion and understanding—to walk with those in need, to comfort them. People need the loving touch, the embrace of a friend. We need someone to reach out to us in troubling times. Reaching out implies doing something, doesn't it? Compassionate people are those who feel the pain of others and *act* to alleviate that pain.

Dr. Bernadine Healy, the current president of the American Red Cross, recently said, "Everyone is asking 'What can I do'? There is much to do in the weeks and months ahead. Reach out to a neighbor, regardless of heritage. Console a grieving friend. Give blood. Volunteer in your community. Make a donation to the charity of your choice. Mostly, *sustain this spirit of America at its best.* This is a time for compassion . . ." (emphasis added).

How right she is. As a pastor, however, I want to ask you to pray and to remember that our greatest source of comfort is God who, Himself, has identified with us in our sorrows and pain. Our God, who is "a Man of sorrows and acquainted with grief." So well He understands our situation, our uncertainty, and our fears and through us is able to comfort others.

Notice how the apostle Paul comments in Second Corinthians on our heavenly Father's understanding of our human condition:

Blessed be the God and Father of our Lord Jesus Christ, the Father of mercies and God of all comfort. (2 Cor. 1:3)

May I say to you who are suffering, who are deeply grieved and hurt over the loss of your loved ones and friends, that God will be your source of comfort and strength. He grieves with you as you bear the awful sense of emptiness and helplessness. He offers you mercy for these dark days. It is His desire to comfort your heart. He is the one "who comforts us in all our affliction" (v. 4). It is His nature to comfort His children.

The Scriptures depict God as a loving father caring for His children as a tender, nurturing nurse and as a mother hen hovering over and protecting her chicks. These metaphors are pictures of a God committed to compassionate care for His children.

A fundamental requisite for those who seek to comfort others is the ability to *forget about self*. It is so easy for us to become enamored of our own affairs and get caught up in our own journey to significance and success.

We must work hard *to put others first*. Who can ever forget images of Mother Teresa in the suburbs of Calcutta pouring out her life for the poor and needy? And what about the self-sacrificing plane passengers who lost their lives while attempting to thwart the hijackers from using the plane as an instrument of further death and destruction?

We must become successful comforters by *being present* while others weep, by sharing a shoulder for others to lean on, and by being a reliable and careful listener. We must be dependable and trustworthy with the thoughts that are shared with us and avoid giving hasty answers or worn-out cliches to those who grieve. Grieving people need the safety of friends who hold them up rather than hold them accountable for what they express in anger and frustration. Yes, there is the great opportunity for us to be channels of mercy and comfort in the name of our Lord.

Do you recall my earlier comments about King David? He refused to be ensnared by fear because he was confident that God was with him and would deliver him from the enemies that pursued him. In Psalm 46 David says, "God is our refuge and strength, A very present help in trouble." This shepherd boy-turned-king learned how to experience the presence of almighty God in the midst of adversity and tragedy. No matter the circumstance, David's bottom line was his confident assurance that God was present in his life.

David's fifty-seventh Psalm has been helpful to me through the years:

Be gracious to me, O God, be gracious to me, for my soul takes refuge in Thee; . . . in the shadow of Thy wings I will take refuge,

until destruction passes by. (Ps. 57:1)

Perhaps some of you are thinking that because I am a minister I have had a life devoid of hardship and tragedy. That would be far from the truth. On many occasions, in the midst of extremely difficult circumstances, I have found myself drawn to that verse as I sought comfort and assurance from God. Here is His promise: when our hearts are so empty and our pain so intense, our hurt so deep and our grief so overwhelming, we are to come to the Father in the shadow of His wings and find a refuge "until destruction passes by."

Mark my words, the destruction, the evil, and the pain will eventually pass! No matter how deeply you hurt, how acute your pain, how hopeless you feel—when you come to your heavenly Father for help and compassion and love, He will be there for you. He will carry you *through* until you are strong enough to stand alone again.

A NATION DRAWS TOGETHER

Because of the recent hijackings, life and the way we do some things may never be the same again. But you can be certain that your heavenly Father will *always* be the same! The eternal God will walk with you the rest of your life. He will enable you to adjust. He will enable you to understand. And, if you so choose, He will enable you to live life more fully than you have before.

God will enable you to respond to the needs of others with compassion and love. Has it amazed you that since the terrorist attacks,

Americans have united to help one another? We have been responding passionately and positively to the needs of others. It is a beautiful thing to see and a beautiful thing to be a part of, indeed.

I am not surprised to see the American flag flying everywhere I look—we are a strong, patriotic nation. Yes I am not surprised, but I am thrilled to see compassion in action—people hugging each other, crying on each other's shoulders, lending aid to one another. No one is concerned about skin color or language or heritage. Our primary concern is *how people can be helped* and how suffering can be alleviated.

What greater evidence can there be that our nation is responding correctly to this tragedy than the magnificent example of the two hundred-fifty firemen and policemen who willingly risked their lives to rescue those trapped in the burning towers? They saved the lives of others but lost their own. The images of the tangled steel ruins are a monument to their devotion to others and to our nation. I hope that one day there will be a permanent national symbol to remind all, who walk by the World Trade Center towers site, of their compassionate sacrifice.

Think about what has happened spontaneously all across this country—people are stepping out of their homes to gather together in communities for candle-lighting ceremonies. Clearly a nerve has been touched. A rawness in our national psyche has been uncovered, and *we need each other*.

For the first time in many a year, we feel emptiness inside and we are calling out to one another. Listen: "Come walk with me . . . let me take your hand . . . do you have time to share this journey? Will God hear my prayers? Where do I find spiritual guidance at a time like this?" We have an opportunity to join our hands and hearts together across America. We are drawn together in a way that is honorable and affirming.

It will take years to discover all the marvelous ways in which Americans have exhibited their compassion and their love during these difficult days. Industries have donated millions of dollars, churches and other organizations have generously contributed, and so have millions of individual Americans—all expressing compassion and love. What an awesome response!

2

Living Fearlessly

There is a second response that is also very important: *We must be courageous to face this tragedy calmly, with determination and without fear.* We are not a fearful people. We do not suddenly give up just because something frightens us. When I was about nine years of age, Pearl Harbor was attacked. The American response was unforgettable. Young men, barely sixteen or seventeen years old, lined up to enlist and to serve. They did not care which branch of service would take them; they only wanted to defend their nation.

When united, this country trembles before no other power. We have a national sense of courage and bravery. We have a heritage of firmness and determination that has carried us through many troubling and dangerous times. I want to remind you of this so that none of us will expect anything less from our nation than a determined, courageous response to the task ahead. Doris Dougherty captured this moment accurately when she said, "No greater tragedy can be found than that of a soul crying out 'It's not fair!' and allowing the cold waters of cynicism to overflow and to drown him." She continues that there is no greater victory than to plunge into these waters where the bottom cannot be felt, but the strong person will "swim until I can!" We may not be able to feel the bottom now, but our country will swim until we do!

In the 1940s America began fighting a war in the Pacific and soon thereafter a war in

Europe as well. Back then, America was not heavily industrialized; we were mostly a nation of farmers. We were unprepared for war, and yet we successfully fought on two fronts for four long years. The cost was devastatingly high, but we were triumphant, which says something about our bravery, determination, and national character.

Over these last few days, I have seen a new spirit of courage and determination across America. Except for a few, this has not been an in-your-face arrogant expression of disdain and self-aggrandizement. On the contrary it is as if a sleeping giant who has been awakened will confidently take his rightful position, fully aware of whom he is and what he can accomplish. People are stepping up to the plate who have been sitting in the shadows with little interest in joining the game. The spirit of courageous King David has gripped the nation, and we are joining him to boldly assert:

> Though a host encamp against me, my heart will not fear. Though war rise against me, In spite of this I shall be confident. (Ps. 27:3)

There may be some reading this book who are fearful, deeply afraid, or overwhelmed with fear. Over the years God has used a special Scripture to help me face periods when rational and irrational fears threatened my confidence and contentment. Read this powerful passage:

> Behold, all those who are angered at you will be shamed and dishonored; Those who contend with you will be as nothing and will perish. You will seek those who quarrel with you, but will not find them, Those

who war with you will be as nothing, and non-existent.

For I am the Lord your God, who upholds your right hand. (ISA. 41:11–13)

We have a right to be a godly people who are fearless. We have a right to be bold and confident for the simple reason that God has promised to intervene in our behalf. Does that mean that we will never suffer consequences? No, it does not. Will we always be free from hardship and adversity? Of course not. It means that when we, as individuals or as a nation, stand sovereign under the protection of God, then we can be assured that He will not fail us. No matter neither the disaster that we face nor the enemy at our gate, with our God we will be triumphant.

We can never know what transpired in the

hearts and minds of those men and women who died in the collapse of the World Trade Center buildings, but I am sure that many, knowing that they were about to die, courageously committed themselves into the arms of a loving God. One whose arms were there to shield them from the steel and rubble and usher them gently to their heavenly reward.

There is an old gospel song by Charles Tindley that states, "We'll understand it better by and by." Only in eternity will we understand some of the mysterious ways of almighty God. Only then will we grasp the significance of His eternal plan that encompasses all of us.

GOD IS IN CONTROL

We have noted that our response to tragedy must be with compassion and concern, and that we must exercise our faith, courage, and confidence in God, who has promised to never leave us or to forsake us. There is a third response. It is a natural thing for those faced with sudden calamity to ask, "*God, why did you allow this disaster?*" We should not ignore this question but instead face the issue. Many would prefer to leave God out of the discussion, as if they fear that He may have an inadequate response. For those of us who know Him as our heavenly Father, however, we are not afraid to face this issue. We know the clear promises of His book and to seek to understand why God permits tragedy is an appropriate response.

Some people believe one should never ask questions of God, even though this is not a biblical position. Courageous King David often commented on his inability to understand the ways of God and, at times, was forthright in his probing questions. We can learn the ways of God by seeking answers to difficult problems and heartaches. But we must not leave God out of the equation!

Consider four categories of people who have a difficult time with this issue:

1. Atheists. They believe our universe is closed, with no possibility of outside influence from any source They believe there is no point in introducing God into any conversation because there is no such being.

2. Those who have a warped, distorted idea of God. Inevitably their perception of God distorts His character in some flagrant way. For example, they accept that He is loving

but reject that He is a God of holiness and justice. They cannot balance these two seeming competing ideas.

3. Those who have an inadequate understanding of Scripture. Many misunderstand the ways of God because they have not studied the Bible and question how He acts and why He allows tragedy and evil in this world.

4. Those who refuse to acknowledge that they are accountable to God. Unfortunately many Americans fall into this category. Many are theists who believe in God but choose to live their lives as though He is absent and uninformed about them and their circumstances.

Here are some sobering questions for every category of people, and I use the word "sobering" very deliberately. Did God know about the attacks before they happened? Yes, He is omniscient or all-knowing. Did God initiate these attacks? No, but He did permit them to happen. If He knew about the attacks, why did He allow them to happen?

Think carefully about these questions. The Scripture says God's throne is established in the heavens and His sovereignty rules over all (see Ps. 103:19). Clearly we are told that God is in charge, He is in control. Nothing happens apart from His knowledge, His understanding, and His power.

If God is not in control, who is? If this tragedy occurred and God could not have stopped it, then somewhere out there is something more powerful than God. This is not the case. Those of us who are believers are convinced by experience and faith that there is no power equal to God in this universe. We believe He is in absolute total control.

This being the case, some will still question, "Why? Why did God allow it to happen?" With all the earnestness in my heart, I respond to you by saying, "You can find out." Please, just ask Him. Prayerfully engage Him with your questions and concerns. He is committed to respond to the open and truthful heart. He is not afraid of your questions. He gives honest answers. As you earnestly and honestly seek Him, I guarantee that He will begin to give you the answers to your questions and, at the same time, start to change and to transform your life. You may even find yourself asking Him: "What do you want to teach me through this series of tragic events?" In my experience God works good out of evil and gives comfort and strength to the most sorrowful heart. That is the kind of God He is.

3

*An Avenger Who
Brings Wrath*

THE ORDINANCES OF GOD

Another correct response we must make in times of tragedy is to *execute our God-given responsibility to discover the perpetrators of these crimes and to bring them to justice.* Our government, with our support, has this responsibility. I am sure that some will ask, "Should we forgive these criminals?" The answer is simple—yes, but they should face the consequences of their deeds.

How profound is the love of God to us, and how amazing the extent of His mercy and grace poured out on sinners. A hymn writer described it this way:

O the deep, deep love of Jesus, vast unmea-
sured, boundless, free; rolling as a mighty
ocean in its fullness over me. (*Hymns II,
InterVaristy Press, 1976, p.25*)

When we experience that forgiving love, however, it does not mean that we escape the consequences of our sins.

Forgiveness never means "no consequences"! A love that does not discipline or
correct is not a genuine love. It is the will of
God, based on the law of God and the Word
of God that our government's mandate includes
the responsibility of bringing to justice those
who deliberately attack innocent people and
bring disaster upon our land.

Romans 13 gives us the background for
the role of the government and how we should
respond to elected officials:

[E]very person be in subjection to the governing authorities. For there is no authority except from God, and those which exist are established by God.

Therefore [whoever] resists authority has opposed the ordinance of God; and they who have opposed will receive condemnation upon themselves. (vv. 1–2)

The teaching of the apostle Paul is clear. We are to acknowledge the authority of government. Our responsibility, unless the authorities ask us to disobey God or participate in immoral actions, is to obey the laws established by our government. If we resist, however, though our reasons may be just and biblically based, we must be prepared to suffer the consequences of our actions. Paul points out that we need not fear properly elected authority, if our actions are good, in verses three and four:

> For rulers are not a cause of fear for good behavior, but for evil . . . [F]or it is a minister of God to you for good. But if you do what is evil, be afraid; for it does not bear the sword for nothing; for it is a minister of God, an avenger who brings wrath upon the one who practices evil.

Our government has an awesome responsibility, and we have an awesome responsibility too. We are called to cooperate with the authorities, to support them, and to pray for them. Our President and his leadership team need the supporting prayers of God's people. Our leaders need wisdom and, more importantly, divine wisdom. We need to pray that while our President consults with those who are there to give him advice, his primary source of counsel will be from the source of wisdom Himself, the omniscient God.

We have a President who is a Christian. He acknowledges his dependence on God, and he has the courage to publicly express his faith without shame or embarrassment. He is a churchgoer—not for show, but because he recognizes the need for Christian fellowship and the importance of being taught the Scriptures, which are able to make us wise. With this in mind *we must support our President with prayer*. Oswald Chambers said, "War is a conflict of wills, either of individuals or of nations." This is what we are facing, a conflict of wills. Our President and our nation need a steely resolve not to buckle for one moment under the oppressive threats of terrorists. This is a sobering moment in our history. Let us support our national government as it brings these terrorists to justice.

4

Discovering the Good

A DIVINE BOUNDARY

There's another response that I think is so very important. I believe *we are to endeavor to discover the good that God will bring from this tragedy.* Some may ask, "How can you even think that anything good could come out of this horrific calamity that has befallen our nation?" When we are felled by tragic events, often we are so wounded that even the most ordinary tasks seem gargantuan in scope, and the thought that one day things will get back to a degree of normalcy seems incomprehensible.

Deep emotional scarring can blind us to the possibility that in the future there will be healing and peace for even the most trauma-tized of souls—but *healing does come*. In fact I know a man in Atlanta who lost two businesses and the love of many of his friends and family, and for years was living in a semi-permanent state of depression. Like the phoenix, however, with God's guidance and blessing, he has risen out of the ashes of despair and, with family alongside him, he has become a beacon of hope to many seeking help in the aftermath of per-sonal tragedy. If you asked this man how he was able to rebound, he would probably refer you to Romans 8:28. This is one of the most familiar passages in the entire Bible:

> And we know that God causes all things to work together for good to those who love God, to those who are called accord-ing to His purpose.

You may say, "But that refers only to those who love God. What about all these traumatized people who don't love him?" First, why not thank God for the millions of Jesus' followers who do love Him and who represent such a strong stabilizing force in the world? If you do not have a meaningful relationship with Jesus at this time, be grateful that there is a worldwide company of believers, the Church, to pray, support, and care for you and others like you.

Second, be thankful that God has established limits by which He decrees the boundaries of men's activities. Make no mistake, His purposes and His authority limit plans of all men. Our Lord has given us freedom of will and choice to the point where he says, "No further." On September 11, 2001, our God allowed and limited the tragedy in New York and Washington, D.C. There was a divine boundary placed upon that contemplated evil.

Some of us became personally enmeshed within the circle of its devastation, losing relatives and friends, emotional stability, and financial security. Others have been swept up in the aftereffects—the tears, the fears, the losses, and the pain. This has been the pattern of life, the ebb and flow of good and evil, since the world began.

Is there not a balance between freedom and license? Any parent can tell how fraught with danger the pathway to manhood is for a growing teenager. How much freedom should be allowed? Will his or her necessary struggle for independence and adulthood be too thwarted by the limits in place for safety and security? These are difficult questions. How much more important is it then for our heavenly Father to exercise His control over the affairs of His world?

LOOK FOR THE GOOD

If it is a good response to the tragedy to look for the good, what do we find?

1. There is a greater sense of unity in America than at any time since the second World War. Eleven months ago, the nation was in a crisis of bitterness over a close presidential election. Some thought the delicate balance of political disagreement had vanished into a cauldron of hate and that the interminable pervasive rancor would never stop. Was it a Japanese Admiral who stated that he was afraid the attack on Pearl Harbor had awakened a sleeping giant? There is no doubt in my mind that this has now happened

in our country. We are awake, and we are united!

2. We have developed a seemingly instantaneous reverence and respect for human life that for many years has been lost in our culture. For example, our nation thrives on competition. We are a sporting nation, and some might even suggest that we have made a god out of sports and of winning at all costs. But in an unthinkable demonstration of respect and reverence for those who lost their lives in New York and Washington, D.C., every major sporting event in our country was canceled for one complete week.

Think about the financial losses—the television revenue, the ticket sales, the lost wages, the empty hotel rooms—all considered secondary to the need for the nation to respect human life.

Can you imagine anything that would shut down a football game or a baseball game, especially during the final series of games to determine the pennant winners? None of us would ever have dreamed anything short of a natural disaster could have caused this to happen. The truth is, there was no presidential decree that all sporting events were to be postponed or canceled, as was done by President Jimmy Carter prior to the staging of the Olympic games in Russia in 1980. On the contrary there was a general consensus that certain activities were no longer appropriate. This attitude speaks of a reverence and a respect for human life that we have not seen before.

3. There is a realization among the general populace that, ultimately, only God can protect our nation. We may search out, round up, incarcerate, and possibly execute those who

committed this outrage, but we know that there will always be others ready to take their place.

Only God can protect America. All our armaments, weaponry, financial strength, material resources, and political will cannot guarantee our protection. That is why it is a critical thing for us to turn our hearts back to God.

4. For the first time in many, many decades people have become more important than profit. It is a good thing to see, in this capitalistic society, corporations giving so generously to the needs of others. Millions of dollars are being donated to relief agencies.

The Salvation Army and the American Red Cross have been inundated with gifts for the New Yorkers who suffered such great losses. The Salvation Army has a divisional headquarters on Fourteenth Street in New York City. From the ninth floor a group of officers with computers and cell phones are continuously locating and distributing food, clothing, and dry goods. From where do these donations come? The generous hearts of Americans. This new kinder, gentler, and more generous spirit becomes all of us. It says something about the real character of the American people, and it says something good.

5. We have become more God-conscious. Publishers tell us that they sell more books on spiritual and religious subjects in times of crisis than they do during normal circumstances. Do you know why? Because when we find ourselves under duress, when our moorings are adrift, we are unable to provide the internal self-assurance that things are going to be okay.

Too often, we are incapacitated by feelings of inadequacy and helplessness—that is why we tend to turn to God in difficult times. And this is not a cop-out or the path of someone who is weak and needs a crutch. God has made us in His image and, therefore, we are most alive and whole when we invite Him to nourish and to succor us along life's journey. If you are feeling helpless or hopeless right now, here is a great prayer to offer: "Father, you know me best, please help me."

This morning, an Atlanta radio station commented on the unusual amount of downtown-area traffic confusion. In all the years I have lived in the metro area, I have never heard a traffic reporter state that the reason for the delays was because there were too many people attending church! May God bless our nation with more and more sensitivity to His presence. Would it not be wonderful if once again His powerful presence would be felt all across our land—in factories, in schools and universities, in corporate offices and state assemblies—wherever people are congregating? May it be so!

6. Another benefit of the crisis, I believe, is that everywhere one goes there is a sense of brokenness and grief that has blanketed our nation like a cloud. Adults and children alike have been affected by the ubiquitous sadness and mourning. Why is this good? Because it is forcing many of us to deal honestly with our feelings.

Parents have an opportunity to communicate with their children, to open doors of understanding and identification. Has your child asked, "Mom and Dad, why were all those people jumping from that building?" "What happens to them after they jump?" "Dad, would you be okay if you had to jump like that?" "Where would you have gone if you died like that?" "Where did those people go?" Such heady and emotive questions require honest, nonevasive answers.

This is a grand opportunity for all of us to deal with the issues of death and dying. We are being forced to face difficult issues, so it gives us an opportunity to consider what types of parents we are. It gives us an occasion for some serious self-evaluation. We can ponder how much time we spend with our families and where they fall on our priority scale.

I felt like weeping as I saw the owner of one of the largest bond-trading companies in the world (with offices at the top of one of the World Trade Center towers) relate his sense of devastation when he realized he had lost most of his work force. Between sobs, he allowed that he and his firm would be changed forever.

He made a public commitment that he was assuming responsibility for all of his employees' families. In describing his situation on that fateful day, he indicated that morning it was his responsibility to drop his child off at school before heading for the office. His life was spared because of a few minutes' delay. All across this land there seems to be a new spirit, a new humility, gentility, if you will. This is a good thing that is strongly supported by the bold assertion of Scripture, which says God hates arrogance but loves a broken and a contrite heart.

WHAT LEGACY WILL YOU LEAVE?

I feel there is a greater sense of things eternal than there has been for a long, long time. I saw a man being interviewed whose father was lost in the collapse of the building. In response to one of the questions, he replied, "I am all right because I know where my father is—he is okay." This son was proclaiming for all the world to see and hear that his father had been a Christian and had lived his life so that his son was proud to be known as his son. This man was affirming confidently that although he was grieving and would continue to do so, he would not grieve as one without hope. On the contrary he was positive that his beloved father was now in the presence of the God he had served so faithfully. He had been left with a godly heritage. In his pain he was comforted.

What more needs to be said? Now is a wonderful time to think not only about the legacy we will leave behind but also our home for eternity. One of my life's constant concerns relates to the legacy that I will leave my children and grandchildren. What have I taught them about life's priorities? Have I lived with integrity? As I have sought to live a life with character, have the positives outweighed the negatives? These questions and a hundred more flood my mind as I think about eternity and how prepared I am to face my heavenly Father.

This is a great time to *get serious about your relationship with God*. Now is the time to stop driving by church—go in. Get your Bible dirty from fingerprints and tears rather than letting it be dusty from lack of use. Search for God and find peace in your soul, rather than seeking for gold and finding poverty in your soul.

5

*A Passion for
God and Country*

A NEW PATRIOTISM

Another good thing flowing from the tragedy is the new spirit of patriotism across the land. A few years ago, with disrespect, some were burning the American flag. And now, with deep respect, we are bearing it! What a change of heart—what a dramatic, transforming time this has been for us. It is so good to hear of men and women digging into their closets and searching through attics to find Old Glory. Many of these flags have particular significance and stir passionate memories for us. That is good too.

We have had enough of the ignorance and ingratitude of those days when rebel hearts rejected our traditional mores and values. In towns and cities across the fruited plain there is evidence of a renewed spirit of patriotism and a renewed spirit of appreciation for all the brave men and women who have preceded us—many of them dying in service of our country.

You can tell how thankful I am for this change of attitude about our flag. This renewed sense of loyalty, devotion, honor, and respect for our country is a good thing.

CHANGES FOR A NATION

This tragedy has also sent a clear and concise message to our government: some things need to be changed. The government must pay more attention to national security concerns. Our life-styles will be affected, our patience and civility will be tested, and we are all going to be inconvenienced *for our own good.* Now that our nation has faced this horrible destruction, it is evident that for us to feel secure again, the government must carefully analyze the various security issues and then act accordingly. Our government must have our support.

President Roosevelt said to the nation, "We have nothing to fear but fear itself." I, however, fear a return to a self-centered, greedy, uncaring, profit-motivated America. I fear a return to the days when our hearts were callous to eternal things and hardened to the needs of our neighbors. We must not forget the precious lessons learned from these tragic days. I pray: Hold fast to us, dear God. Please do not leave us alone. Do not leave us to our own devices. May the date September 11, 2001, be forever a turning point in the life of this nation.

A SIMPLE PLAN

We have discussed how we as individuals and as a nation should respond to the worst single-day tragedy that has ever befallen our country. We have considered together how to turn our faces up to God and our hands out to help our fellow man. Finally we must discuss what may be the most beneficial thing to come from the attacks—a returning to God's simple, yet profound, plan for our lives.

For some of you, however, there is a fundamental problem with this plan. You feel alienated from God. Frankly, years ago, before I became a minister, I felt the same way before someone shared with me the good news, the marvelous story of God's eternal plan to help us all reconnect with Him. God created the world through His unprecedented power and authority. He created humans and allowed us to enjoy His beautiful world. But our forefathers messed up, and we have continued to do the same ever since. We rebelled against His principles and laws, and we still do so. In other words we sin.

Inevitably sin leads us away from God and pushes us to do our own thing. As a result we become more self-reliant and less aware of our need of God. When tragedy comes across our paths, as it always does, we do not have the resources within ourselves to bring peace to our troubled hearts. This is good, because it usually opens a window to our souls, a window that our loving Father can open and use to make contact with us again.

Of course I am talking in generalities, but I do this to show that His plan *does* include you. No matter how far away from Him you have traveled, He still knows, understands, and loves you. He can open the window to your heart. All that is required is your permission. When you give the word, He will act. Then, you will learn that His Son, Jesus, came into our world to live and to die as one of us, yet still he retained His divinity. Amazing, isn't it? Further, as a sinless man, Jesus was killed because our ancestors thought he was a criminal, a fake Christ. Yes, they thought he was an imposter—not the real Son of God. But after his death he did what no other person has ever done: by the power of God, he rose out of death. In doing this he triumphed over it, that nasty reality we all seem to fear. He went back to his Father in heaven and now prays for us and waits to meet us when we die.

There is only one sticking point. God requires us to recognize that we cannot ever be good enough to make it to heaven on our own. Why would Jesus have had to suffer if we could be good enough? No, we are required to ask for His mercy, to confess our sins, and to trust Him for our salvation. That, my friend, is the best piece of good news you will ever hear. I hope that out of these dark, tragic days, you will find inner peace and forgiveness. They are the wonderful gifts of God.

MOBILIZE FOR PRAYER

Since September 11, 2001, the Dow Jones Industrial average has lost 1,400 points and $1.4 trillion of wealth. Almost all major American airlines have been forced to give pink slips to approximately 100,000 workers, and more than eighty of our leading economists now believe we are in a financial recession.

The latest estimates indicate that the cleanup in New York City will take close to one year, and the federal government has created a $40 billion fund to rebuild the Pentagon and to provide the necessary funds for war preparations and the rebuilding in New York. Armed Forces reserve units are being called to active duty, and ships and planes are leaving our shores for unspecified locations for undetermined amounts of time. We are a nation in crisis. A nation that must, in the words of military historian Paul Fussell, have "a stiffening of national resolve." Most importantly, however, as people of faith, we must continue to mobilize ourselves to steadfastly work and pray for the nation. Now is the time for fervent prayers and ardent patriotism, for passionate giving and selfless living. It is the opportunity of a lifetime *to make a change*—to be a different person and a different people.

We have an opportunity, by faith, to believe in each other for a better future; to forgive each other for past wrongs; and to go the extra mile for friend and enemy alike. Out of tragedy can come triumph.

About the Author

Dr. Charles Stanley is pastor of the 15,000-member First Baptist Church in Atlanta, Georgia. He is well-known through his In Touch radio and television ministry to thousands internationally and is the author of many books, including *On Holy Ground, Our Unmet Needs, Into His Presence, Enter His Gates, The Source of My Strength, The Reason for My Hope, How to Listen to God,* and *How to Handle Adversity.*

Dr. Stanley received his bachelor of arts degree from the University of Richmond, his bachelor of divinity degree from Southwestern Theological Seminary, and his master's and doctor's degrees from Luther Rice Seminary. He has twice been elected president of the Southern Baptist Convention.

Other Books by Charles Stanley from
Thomas Nelson Publishers